COMMON CORE LANGUAGE ARTS 4 Today

Daily Skill Practice

Grade K

Jennifer Taylor Geck

Carson-Dellosa Publishing, LLC
Greensboro, North Carolina

Credits

Content Editor: Jennifer B. Stith
Copy Editor: Beatrice Allen

 Visit *carsondellosa.com* for correlations to Common Core State, national, and Canadian provincial standards.

Carson-Dellosa Publishing, LLC
PO Box 35665
Greensboro, NC 27425 USA
carsondellosa.com

ISBN 978-1-62442-603-2

03-160141151

Table of Contents

Introduction 4

Building a Reading Environment 5

Writing Strategies 6

Common Core State Standards
Alignment Matrix 7

Week 1 9

Week 2 11

Week 3 13

Week 4 15

Week 5 17

Week 6 19

Week 7 21

Week 8 23

Week 9 25

Week 10 27

Week 11 29

Week 12 31

Week 13 33

Week 14 35

Week 15 37

Week 16 39

Week 17 41

Week 18 43

Week 19 45

Week 20 47

Week 21 49

Week 22 51

Week 23 53

Week 24 55

Week 25 57

Week 26 59

Week 27 61

Week 28 63

Week 29 65

Week 30 67

Week 31 69

Week 32 71

Week 33 73

Week 34 75

Week 35 77

Week 36 79

Week 37 81

Week 38 83

Week 39 85

Week 40 87

Answer Key 89

Common Core Language Arts 4 Today: Daily Skill Practice is a perfect supplement to any classroom language arts curriculum. Students' reading skills will grow as they work on comprehension, fluency, vocabulary, and decoding. Students' writing skills will improve as they work on elements of writing, writing structure, genre, parts of speech, grammar, and spelling, as well as the writing process.

This book covers 40 weeks of daily practice. Three questions a day for four days a week will provide students with ample practice in language arts skills. A separate assessment is included for the fifth day of each week.

Various skills and concepts are reinforced throughout the book through activities that align to the Common Core State Standards. To view these standards, please see the Common Core State Standards Alignment Matrix on pages 7 and 8.

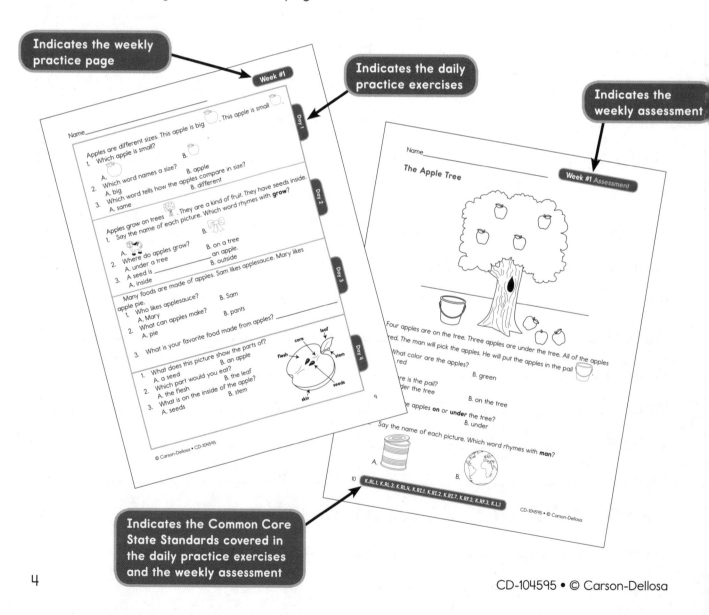

Indicates the weekly practice page

Indicates the daily practice exercises

Indicates the weekly assessment

Indicates the Common Core State Standards covered in the daily practice exercises and the weekly assessment

Building a Reading Environment

A positive reading environment is essential to fostering successful readers. When building a reading environment, think of students' physical, emotional, and cognitive needs.

Physical Environment
- Make the physical reading environment inviting and comfortable. Create a reading corner with comfortable chairs, floor pillows, a rug, enticing lighting, etc.
- Give students access to a variety of texts by providing books, magazines, newspapers, and Internet access. Read signs, ads, posters, menus, pamphlets, labels, boxes, and more!
- Provide regularly scheduled independent reading time in class. Encourage students to read at home. They can read to a younger sibling or read anything of interest such as comic books, children's and sports magazines, chapter books, etc.
- Set a positive example. Make sure students see you reading too!

Emotional Environment
- Learn about students' reading habits, preferences, strengths, and weaknesses. Then, provide books that address these issues.
- Help students create connections with text. Facilitate connections by activating prior knowledge, examining personal meaning, and respecting personal reflections.
- Give students the opportunity to choose titles to read. This will give them a sense of ownership, which will engage them in the text and sustain interest.
- Create a safe environment for exploring and trying new things. Foster a feeling of mutual respect for reading abilities and preferences.
- Require students to read at an appropriate reading level. Text in any content area, including leisure reading, should not be too easy or too difficult.
- Have all students participate in reading, regardless of their reading levels. Try to include slower readers and be sure to give them time to finish before moving on or asking questions.
- Be enthusiastic about reading! Talk about books you love and share your reading experiences and habits. Your attitude about reading is contagious!

Cognitive Environment
- Regardless of the grade level, read aloud to students every day. Reading aloud not only provides a good example but also lets students practice their listening skills.
- Help students build their vocabularies to make their reading more successful. Create word walls, personal word lists, mini-dictionaries, and graphic organizers.
- Read for different purposes. Reading a novel requires different skills than reading an instruction manual. Teach students the strategies needed to comprehend these different texts.
- Encourage students to talk about what and how they read. Use journal writing, literature circles, class discussions, conferences, conversations, workshops, seminars, and more.
- Writing and reading are inherently linked. Students can examine their own writing through reading and examine their reading skills by writing. Whenever possible, facilitate the link between reading and writing.

Choose a **topic** for your writing.
- What am I writing about?

Decide on a **purpose** for writing.
- Why am I writing this piece?
- What do I hope the audience will learn from reading this piece?

Identify your **audience**.
- Who am I writing to?

Decide on a writing **style**.
- Expository—gives information or explains facts or ideas
- Persuasive—tries to talk someone into something
- Narrative—tells a story
- Descriptive—presents a clear picture of a person, place, thing, or idea

Decide on a **genre**—essay, letter, poetry, autobiography, fiction, or nonfiction.

Decide on a **point of view**—first person, second person, or third person.

Brainstorm by listing or drawing your main ideas.

Use a graphic organizer to **organize** your thoughts.

Revise, revise, revise!
- Use **descriptive words**.
- Use **transitions** and linking expressions.
- Use a **variety of sentence structures**.
- **Elaborate** with facts and details.
- Group your ideas into **paragraphs**.
- **Proofread** for capitalization, punctuation, and spelling.

Common Core State Standards Alignment Matrix

STANDARD	W1	W2	W3	W4	W5	W6	W7	W8	W9	W10	W11	W12	W13	W14	W15	W16	W17	W18	W19	W20
K.RL.1	●	●	●	●	●	●	●	●	●	●		●	●	●			●	●	●	
K.RL.2																				
K.RL.3	●	●	●	●	●	●	●	●	●	●		●	●	●	●		●	●		
K.RL.4	●		●	●		●		●	●				●					●		
K.RL.5																				
K.RL.6					●	●						●								
K.RL.7				●	●	●		●	●			●	●				●	●	●	
K.RI.1	●	●	●	●	●		●	●			●		●	●	●	●	●		●	●
K.RI.2	●			●			●	●	●	●	●	●		●	●	●	●		●	●
K.RI.3			●								●	●		●			●			
K.RI.4		●					●					●		●	●	●	●		●	●
K.RI.5												●								
K.RI.6												●								
K.RI.7	●	●		●			●								●	●			●	●
K.RI.9																				
K.RF.2	●	●	●	●	●	●	●	●	●	●	●	●	●	●				●		●
K.RF.3	●	●	●	●			●				●				●	●		●	●	●
K.RF.4	●	●	●	●	●	●	●	●	●	●	●	●					●	●	●	●
K.W.1	●	●			●		●		●			●					●	●	●	
K.W.2				●				●								●	●			●
K.W.3		●		●	●	●	●	●						●		●	●	●		
K.W.8				●	●		●		●	●									●	
K.L.1	●					●	●			●		●	●	●					●	
K.L.2			●					●			●									
K.L.4		●	●	●		●	●		●	●	●			●			●	●		●	●
K.L.5	●			●		●		●	●		●		●			●	●	●	●		●
K.L.6																●				

W = Week

STANDARD	W21	W22	W23	W24	W25	W26	W27	W28	W29	W30	W31	W32	W33	W34	W35	W36	W37	W38	W39	W40
K.RL.1	●		●	●	●	●	●	●	●	●	●	●	●	●	●	●	●	●		●
K.RL.2											●									
K.RL.3	●		●	●	●	●	●	●	●	●	●	●	●	●	●	●	●	●		●
K.RL.4	●			●			●	●			●		●		●		●	●		●
K.RL.5																	●			
K.RL.6																				
K.RL.7			●				●	●	●		●	●								●
K.RI.1	●	●		●	●	●	●	●	●	●		●	●	●	●	●		●	●	
K.RI.2	●	●		●	●	●	●	●	●	●		●	●	●	●	●		●	●	
K.RI.3	●					●				●				●	●	●				
K.RI.4		●		●				●	●	●		●		●	●			●	●	
K.RI.5									●											
K.RI.6																				
K.RI.7		●						●						●				●		
K.RI.9			●						●											
K.RF.2		●	●	●	●		●	●		●	●	●	●		●	●			●	
K.RF.3		●	●		●		●	●	●	●	●			●			●	●	●	
K.RF.4	●	●	●	●	●	●	●	●	●	●	●	●	●	●	●	●	●	●	●	●
K.W.1			●	●		●			●	●							●		●	
K.W.2	●						●			●					●			●		●
K.W.3	●	●	●		●		●		●		●	●	●			●	●	●	●	●
K.W.8	●			●							●	●	●	●		●		●		
K.L.1	●		●			●	●	●					●					●	●	●
K.L.2		●	●		●															
K.L.4	●	●	●					●	●	●				●					●	
K.L.5	●			●			●		●		●	●	●		●		●			●
K.L.6																				

W = Week

Name_____

Apples are different sizes. This apple is big . This apple is small .

1. Which apple is small?

A.   B.

2. Which word names a size?

A. big   B. apple

3. Which word tells how the apples compare in size?

A. same   B. different

Apples grow on trees [tree]. They are a kind of fruit. They have seeds inside.

1. Say the name of each picture. Which word rhymes with **grow**?

A. [cow]   B. [bow]

2. Where do apples grow?

A. under a tree   B. on a tree

3. A seed is _____ an apple.

A. inside   B. outside

Many foods are made of apples. Sam likes applesauce. Mary likes apple pie.

1. Who likes applesauce?

A. Mary   B. Sam

2. What can apples make?

A. pie   B. pants

3. What is your favorite food made from apples? _____

1. What does this picture show the parts of?

A. a seed   B. an apple

2. Which part would you eat?

A. the flesh   B. the leaf

3. What is on the inside of the apple?

A. seeds   B. stem

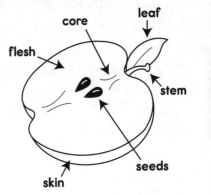

The Apple Tree

Four apples are on the tree. Three apples are under the tree. All of the apples are red. The man will pick the apples. He will put the apples in the pail .

1. What color are the apples?
   A. red   B. green

2. Where is the pail?
   A. under the tree   B. on the tree

3. Are more apples **on** or **under** the tree?
   A. on   B. under

4. Say the name of each picture. Which word rhymes with **man**?

   A.   B.

Name_____

Firefighters use tools to help them. The fire truck gets them to the fire. The hose helps put out the fire. Helmets help keep them safe.

1. Which is not a tool firefighters use?

    A.   B.

2. Draw two tools firefighters use.

3. Would you like to be a firefighter? Tell why or why not.

A fire truck is red. It has a loud siren. The truck holds the ladder.

1. What makes the fire truck loud?

    A. the ladder   B. the siren

2. Say the name of each picture. Which word has the **short e** sound as in **bed**?

    A.   B.

3. Underline the sentence that tells about the siren.

Matches and lighters are not toys. Adults are the only ones who should use these tools. They are used to start fires.

1. Which word means the same as **adult**?

    A. grown-up   B. child

2. Tell a friend what might happen if matches or lighters were used as toys.

3. Matches and lighters are _____.

    A. not toys   B. not tools

Ms. Tang's class had a fire drill. The bell rang. They walked outside in a line.

1. Which word rhymes with **rang**?

    A. ring   B. fang

2. Where did the class walk?

    A. outside   B. to the library

3. Which class had a fire drill?

    A. Mr. Taylor's   B. Ms. Tang's

Day 1

Day 2

Day 3

Day 4

Exit to Safety

Kayla and her mom smell smoke. They crawl to the door. It is hot. Kayla's mom helps Kayla use the window to get outside. They call 911 for help.

1. How did the door feel?
   A. cold   B. hot

2. Who is with Kayla?
   A. her mom   B. her dad

3. Why did they call 911?
   A. They need help.   B. They are hungry.

4. Which word begins with the **sm** sound as in **smoke**?
   A. smile   B. swim

Name_____

Sara lives in an apartment building. She rides the elevator to her home. Sara's home is on the top floor.

1. How does Sara get to her home?
   A. rides an elevator   B. uses the backdoor
2. What kind of home does Sara live in?
   A. a house   B. an apartment
3. Write two small words you can find in the word **apartment**.

   _____   _____

Jackson's house has many rooms. He likes the kitchen. He likes to play games at the table. He also enjoys helping his mom bake cookies.

1. What kind of home does Jackson live in?
   A. a house   B. a tent
2. Which word means the same as **enjoy**?
   A. jump   B. like
3. What does Jackson help his mom do?
   A. clean   B. bake cookies

There are many kinds of homes. Condos, houses, and apartments are all types of homes. Most homes have a kitchen, a bathroom, and one or more bedrooms.

1. Which is a type of home?   A. mouse   B. condo
2. What do most homes have?   A. bathroom   B. play room
3. Say the name of each picture. Which word has the **long o** sound as in **home**?

A.   B.

Ben lives in the mountains. His home is made of logs. It is called a cabin. He loves to play in his yard.

1. What is Ben's home made of?   A. [image]   B. [image]
2. What kind of home does he live in?
   A. an apartment   B. a cabin
3. Say the name of each picture. Which word rhymes with **yard**?

A.   B.

City Homes and Country Homes

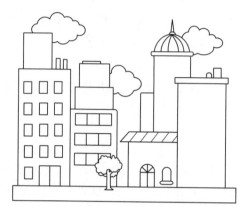

Homes in cities are different from homes in the country. Many people in cities live in apartments. They do not have yards. Homes in the country often have space between them.

1. Where do people in cities often live?
    A. log cabins   B. apartments

2. Which word rhymes with **space**?
    A. race   B. ship

3. Karen lives far away from her neighbor Jim. Where does she live?
    A. the country   B. a city

4. Describe a home in the country. _____

_____

K.RL.1, K.RL.3, K.RL.4, K.RI.1, K.RI.3, K.RF.2, K.RF.3, K.RF.4, K.L.2, K.L.4 CD-104595 • © Carson-Dellosa

Name_____

Firefighters help keep us safe. They ride in a fire truck. They put out fires with hoses.

1. What do firefighters ride in?
   A. a car   B. a truck
2. Say the name of each picture. Which word has the **long a** sound as in **safe**?

   A.   B.
3. Which is used to put out fires?   A. hose   B. helmet

Jane's dad is a nurse. He works at a hospital. He helps sick people get well.

1. Who is a nurse?
   A. Jane's mom   B. Jane's dad
2. Who do nurses help?
   A. lost people   B. sick people
3. Which word is the opposite of **sick**?
   A. ill   B. well

Mr. Kim is our mail carrier. He drives a mail truck. He puts mail in our mailbox.

1. What is Mr. Kim's job?
   A. teacher   B. mail carrier
2. Say the name of each picture. Which word rhymes with **mail**?

   A.   B.
3. Draw one thing a mail carrier does.

Police officers help our town. Some drive police cars and some ride horses. They all work to keep us safe.

1. What do some police officers ride?   A.   B.
2. Say the name of each picture. Which word has the same **ow** sound as in **town**?

   A.   B.
3. Tell one way police officers keep us safe.

Community Helpers

Many people are community helpers. Some workers, such as doctors, firefighters, and police officers, keep us safe and healthy. Librarians and teachers help people learn. Garbage collectors and school custodians help keep things clean. All community helpers work to make our communities better.

1. Police officers keep us _____.
   A. sad   B. safe

2. School custodians help keep things _____.
   A. clean   B. sick

3. Who helps you learn new things?
   A. a mail carrier   B. a teacher

4. Draw a picture of a community helper and show one way he or she helps the community.

Name_____

In autumn, leaves turn different colors. Some turn red, while others turn yellow, orange, or brown. The leaves fall from the trees onto the ground.

1. What color do some leaves turn?
   A. blue   B. orange
2. In what season do the leaves change colors?
   A. autumn   B. winter
3. Say the name of each picture. Which word rhymes with **fall**?

A.   B.

Marc loves autumn. He likes to collect leaves. His favorite leaves are red.
1. Whom is the story about?
   A. Marc   B. Tom
2. What does Marc like to do?
   A. pick apples   B. collect leaves
3. Draw a picture of what Marc's favorite leaf would look like.

Hannah and her sister raked leaves. They raked the leaves into two large piles. They ran and jumped into the piles.
1. Who helps Hannah rake?
   A. her dad   B. her sister
2. How many piles do they rake?
   A. one   B. two
3. Say the name of each picture. Which word rhymes with **ran**?

A.   B.

Cody's dad has an apple farm. In autumn, his dad picks apples from the trees. They sell the apples.

1. What grows on the farm?   A.   B.

2. Where do Cody and his dad live?   A.   B.

3. Write one sentence about what they do with the apples.

_____

Trees

Trees change over time. In spring, buds sprout, and leaves grow. Summertime is when leaves are dark green. In autumn, leaves change colors. In winter, trees have few or no leaves.

1. When do buds sprout?
   A. autumn   B. spring

2. What season comes after summer?
   A. autumn   B. winter

3. Underline the word in the story that begins with the **gr** sound as in **grow**.

4. Draw a picture of your favorite season.

Name_____

Nate's mom took Nate to a pumpkin patch. They looked at all of the pumpkins. They each picked a pumpkin to bring home.

1. What is the setting?
   A. a pumpkin patch   B. school
2. Which word means the same as **pick**?
   A. choose   B. jump
3. How do you think Nate felt?
   A. scared   B. happy

Liz wanted to carve a pumpkin. She used a marker to draw a silly face. Her dad used a knife to carve it.

1. Who helped Liz?
   A. her dad   B. her sister
2. What did Liz use to draw a face on her pumpkin?
   A. a marker   B. a crayon
3. Draw a picture of Liz's pumpkin.

Pumpkins can be eaten in different ways. Mom likes pumpkin seeds. Dad likes pumpkin muffins. I think pumpkin pie is the best.

1. Who likes pumpkin muffins?
   A. Mom   B. Dad
2. Is a girl telling the story?
   A. yes   B. no   C. cannot tell
3. What is different about Mom and Dad? Write a sentence.

_____

Mario and Dan each have a pumpkin. Mario's is small and white. Dan's pumpkin is large, round, and orange.

1. Who has an orange pumpkin?
   A. Mario   B. Dan
2. Which word has the same number of syllables as **pumpkin**?
   A. seed   B. wagon
3. Underline the color words in the story.

Pumpkins

Seth's class weighed a pumpkin. They used string to measure it. Then, they cut it open and counted the seeds.

1. What did Seth's class study?
    A. apples   B. pumpkins

2. In this story, what does it mean to **measure**?
    A. to tell the size   B. to tell the color

3. Which word means the opposite of **open**?
    A. closed   B. up

4. What was the last step?
    A. weighing the pumpkin   B. counting the seeds

K.RL.1, K.RL.3, K.RL.4, K.RL.6, K.RL.7, K.RF.2, K.RF.4, K.W.3, K.L.1, K.L.4, K.L.5   CD-104595 • © Carson-Dellosa

Spiders have eight legs. Their legs help them climb. They also use their legs to smell.

1. How many legs do spiders have?
   A. two   B. eight
2. Which word has the **short e** sound as in **leg**?
   A. net   B. tree
3. What is the topic?
   A. spider legs   B. spiderwebs

Spiders make silk. Some may spin webs from the silk. The webs are sticky.

1. What are spiderwebs made from?
   A. silk   B. yarn
2. **Sticky** tells how the web _____.
   A. smells   B. feels
3. Which word is more than one?
   A. web   B. webs

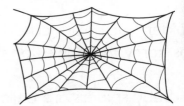

Jacob has a pet spider. He is black and hairy. The spider's name is Webby.

1. Who has a pet spider?
   A. Jacob   B. Webby
2. What color is the spider?
   A. brown   B. black
3. Would you like a pet spider? Why or why not?

_____

Many spiders use webs to catch food. These spiders eat flies and bugs. The bugs get stuck on the sticky webs.

1. What do spiders eat?

   A.   B.
2. What do they use to catch their food?
   A. legs   B. webs
3. Which word is more than one?
   A. bug   B. bugs

Spiderlings

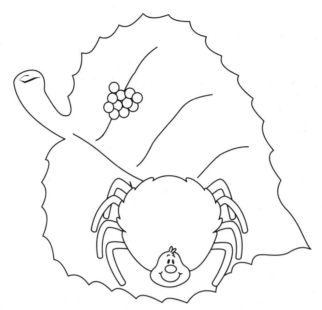

Spider babies are called spiderlings. They hatch from eggs. Many spider moms carry the babies on their backs.

1. Baby spiders are called _____.
   A. spideys   B. spiderlings

2. Say the name of each picture. Which word rhymes with **hatch**?

   A.   B.

3. Where do spider moms carry their babies?
   A. on their backs   B. in their arms

4. Draw a picture of another animal that hatches from an egg.

A gray squirrel lives in Alan's yard. The squirrel sleeps in the big tree. He uses his tail to stay warm.

1. What color is the squirrel?
   A. gray   B. brown
2. What keeps him warm?
   A. his tail   B. a blanket
3. Which word is the opposite of **big**?
   A. large   B. little

The big squirrel chased the small squirrel. They ran up and down the trees. The little squirrel hid behind a bush.

1. Say the name of each picture. Which word rhymes with **big**?

   A.   B.
2. What is the setting of the story? A. outside   B. inside
3. Which punctuation mark do the sentences end with?
   A. !   B. .

Many squirrels collect acorns. They hide them in the trees and ground. They eat the nuts in winter.

1. What do they do with acorns?
   A. play with them   B. hide them
2. Where might a squirrel hide an acorn?
   A. in a tree   B. behind the chair
3. Draw a picture of a squirrel in winter.

There are many kinds of squirrels. Most have big eyes and bushy tails. They eat nuts, seeds, and fruit.

1. Squirrels' eyes are _____.
   A. big   B. little
2. Say the name of each picture. Which word has the **long a** sound as in **tail**?

   A.   B.
3. What do squirrels eat?   A. seeds   B. leaves

Small Squirrels

Chipmunks are small squirrels. They have stripes. They carry food in their cheeks.

1. Where do chipmunks carry their food?
   A. in their hands   B. in their cheeks

2. Small squirrels are called _____.
   A. chipmunks   B. rats

3. Chipmunks have _____.
   A. spots   B. stripes

4. Draw how a chipmunk might look after it has found food.

 K.RL.1, K.RL.3, K.RL.4, K.RL.7, K.RI.1, K.RI.2, K.RI.7, K.RF.2, K.RF.3, K.RF.4, K.W.3, K.L.2, K.L.5

Liam's pet likes to swim. He lives in a glass bowl. His pet is small and orange.
1. What does Liam's pet like to do?
    A. dig   B. swim
2. Draw a picture of Liam's pet.

3. What kind of pet would you like to have?

    _____

Day 1

Emma has a hamster. He is small and brown. He sleeps during the day and plays at night.
1. **Small** and **brown** tell what about the hamster?
    A. what he eats   B. how he looks
2. Which word is a color word like **brown**?
    A. red   B. book
3. Which word is the opposite of **small**?
    A. little   B. large

Day 2

Ava wants a dog. Her mom and dad find one at the animal shelter. Ava names her dog Bud.
1. What kind of pet does Ava want?
    A. a cat   B. a dog
2. Who gets her a pet?   A. her mom and dad   B. Bud
3. Number the events in order from 1 to 3.
    _____ Ava's parents find a dog at the animal shelter.
    _____ Ava names the dog Bud.
    _____ Ava wants a dog.

Day 3

Zach has a kitten. Her name is Sandy. Sandy likes to play with string.
1. What is the kitten's name?
    A. Zach   B. Sandy
2. Which is the kitten's toy?
    A. string   B. ball
3. Is Sandy a boy or a girl?
    A. boy   B. girl

Day 4

Pet Stores

Pet stores sell things for pets. They sell food, toys, and cages. Some pet stores sell pets such as fish and birds.

1. Which can be found at a pet store?
   A. cat food   B. sleds

2. Which word rhymes with **sell**?
   A. map   B. well

3. Where can you buy a bird?
   A. pet store   B. shoe store

4. Which word means the same as **store**?
   A. bag   B. shop

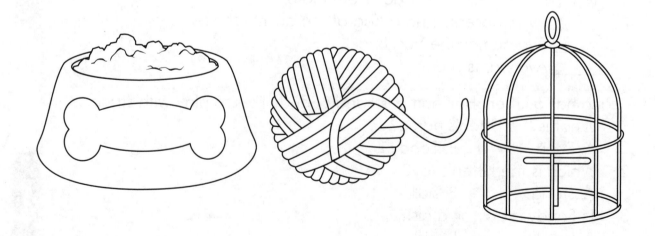

Sarah lives with her mom and grandma. Her grandma is her mom's mother. They are a family.

1. Who does Sara live with?
   A. Mom and Dad   B. Mom and Grandma
2. Which word means the same as **mom**?
   A. mother   B. family
3. Who is the oldest in Sarah's family?
   A. Sarah   B. her grandma

Day 1

Ethan has two brothers. He has an older brother and a younger brother. They all love to play baseball.

1. How many brothers does Ethan have?
   A. two   B. three
2. What do they like to do together?
   A. play football   B. play baseball
3. **Baseball** is a compound word. Which is another compound word?

   A. ladybug   B. mitten

Day 2

Zoe's aunt just had a baby. His name is Zach. Zach is Zoe's cousin.

1. Who had a baby?
   A. Zoe's aunt   B. Zoe
2. What is the baby's name?
   A. Zoe   B. Zach
3. Draw a picture of someone in your family.

Day 3

Jon lives with his mom, dad, and sister. Jon and his sister are twins. They were born on the same day.

1. Who is Jon's twin?
   A. Jon's dad   B. Jon's sister
2. Who was born on the same day as Jon?
   A. his sister   B. his mom
3. How many people are in Jon's family?
   A. three   B. four

Day 4

Families

Families do not all have the same number of people. Some families have more than one child. Some have only one child. Families are made up of people who love you.

1. True or false? Families always have four people in them.
   A. true   B. false

2. Which word is more than one?
   A. person   B. people

3. Underline the number word in the story.

4. Draw a picture of your family.

 K.RL.1, K.RL.3, K.RI.2, K.RF.2, K.RF.4, K.W.8, K.L.1, K.L.4

Turkeys

Turkeys are a kind of bird. Some are brown. They have tail feathers.

1. What color are some turkeys?
   A. green   B. brown
2. Another meaning of **kind** is _____.
   A. nice   B. type
3. Say the name of each picture. Which word rhymes with **tail**?

   A.   B.

Male turkeys are called Tom Turkeys. Girl turkeys are called hens. Hens lay eggs.

1. Hens are _____.
   A. girl turkeys   B. boy turkeys
2. Which lays eggs?   A. tom turkeys   B. hens
3. Say the name of each picture. Which word begins with the **h** sound as in **hen**?

   A.   B.

Wild turkeys live in the woods. They have dark feathers. The feathers help them hide in the woods.

1. Where do wild turkeys live?
   A. on farms   B. in the woods
2. Which word is the opposite of **dark**?   A. light   B. night
3. Say the name of each picture. Which word has the same **oo** sound as in **woods**?

   A.   B.

Wild turkeys spend the day looking for food. They eat nuts, seeds, and small bugs. At night, turkeys sleep in trees.

1. When do turkeys eat?
   A. daytime   B. nighttime
2. Where do wild turkeys sleep?
   A. in beds   B. in trees
3. Which food do turkeys eat?
   A. fish   B. nuts

Turkeys

Male turkeys gobble. The sound is loud. It can be heard one mile away. Female turkeys do not gobble. Instead, they cluck.

1. Which sound do female turkeys make?
   A. gobble   B. cluck

2. Which word describes a **gobble**?
   A. loud   B. quiet

3. Which word is the contraction for **do not**?
   A. didn't   B. don't

4. How far away can a gobble be heard?
   A. 10 miles   B. one mile

K.RI.1, K.RI.2, K.RI.3, K.RI.4, K.RF.2, K.RF.3, K.RF.4, K.L.2, K.L.4, K.L.5   CD-104595 • © Carson-Dellosa

Each Thanksgiving, Liza's family drives to Grandma's house. They spend time with their aunts, uncles and cousins. Grandma cooks a big dinner.

1. When does Liza's family drive to her Grandma's?
   A. Mother's Day   B. Thanksgiving
2. Who cooks Thanksgiving dinner?
   A. Liza   B. Liza's grandma
3. Whom does Liza see at Thanksgiving?
   A. her cousins   B. her teachers

Day 1

Sam's favorite Thanksgiving food is pumpkin pie. His dad likes turkey. Mom makes both.

1. What is Sam's favorite food at Thanksgiving?
   A. pumpkin pie   B. turkey
2. Draw a picture of your favorite Thanksgiving food.

3. Which word is more than one?
   A. pie   B. pies

Day 2

At Thanksgiving, Ty's family tells what they are thankful for. Ty is thankful for his family. He is also thankful for his new dog, Max.

1. Who is Max?
   A. Ty's brother   B. Ty's dog
2. Say the name of each picture. Which word rhymes with **tell**?

   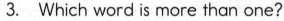

   A.   B.

3. What are you thankful for? _____

Day 3

Thanksgiving is a special day for many families. Some families go to parades, and others watch football. Most families enjoy eating a special meal together.

1. What day is special for many families?
   A. Friday   B. Thanksgiving
2. What do some families like to do?
   A. watch football   B. read
3. Tell a friend what you like to do with your family at Thanksgiving.

Day 4

Thanksgiving

Cara wants to read a Thanksgiving book. She finds these two books at the library.

 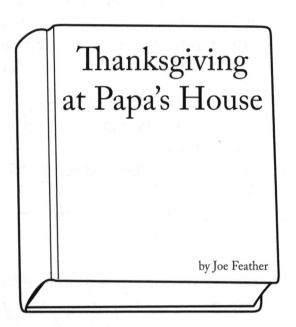

1. Who writes the book?
   A. the author   B. the illustrator

2. Who is the author of *The First Thanksgiving*?
   A. Jan Candle   B. Joe Feather

3. Which book is fiction (make-believe)?
   A. *The First Thanksgiving*   B. *Thanksgiving at Papa's House*

4. Draw what the cover picture might look like for *Thanksgiving at Papa's House*.

 K.RL.1, K.RL.3, K.RL.6, K.RL.7, K.RI.1, K.RI.2, K.RI.3, K.RI.5, K.RI.6, K.RF.2, K.RF.4, K.W.1, K.L.1   CD-104595 • © Carson-Dellosa

Luke plays baseball. He uses the bat to hit the ball. He likes to run around the bases.

1. What does Luke use to play baseball?
   A. a bat   B. a net
2. Which word rhymes with **hit**?
   A. hat   B. mitt
3. Which word is more than one?
   A. base   B. bases

Tim likes to swim. He is on his school swim team. He has won two medals for swimming.

1. Who is the main character?
   A. Tom   B. Tim
2. What does Tim like to do?
   A. swim   B. run
3. Which word is the opposite of **won**?
   A. lost   B. go

Sophia likes to run. She and her dad run every morning. She has her first race on Saturday.

1. Whom does Sophia run with?
   A. her mom   B. her dad
2. When does she run?
   A. in the morning   B. at night
3. When is her first race?
   A. Sunday   B. Saturday

Football players wear uniforms. Each shirt has the player's name and number on it. They also wear helmets.

1. Whom is the paragraph about?
   A. soccer players   B. football players
2. What is written on each player's shirt?
   A. his number   B. his age
3. Draw what your football shirt might look like.

PE Class

Dan's PE teacher lets the class play sports. Last week, they played tennis. This week, they are playing soccer. Dan hopes that they will play basketball next week.

1. Who teaches Dan about different sports?
   A. his friends   B. his PE teacher

2. What sport did they play first?
   A. basketball   B. tennis

3. What sport are they playing this week?
   A. soccer   B. tennis

4. What does Dan want to play next?
   A. basketball   B. football

K.RL.1, K.RL.3, K.RL.4, K.RL.7, K.RF.2, K.RF.4, K.W.3, K.L.1, K.L.5   CD-104595 • © Carson-Dellosa

Name_____

Liz and her family love Christmas. They hang their stockings by the fireplace. They put gifts under the tree.

1. What holiday does Liz celebrate?
    A. Kwanzaa   B. Christmas
2. Where does Liz's family hang their stockings?
    A. under the tree   B. by the fireplace
3. Which word is more than one?
    A. gift   B. gifts

Day 1

Micah's family celebrates Hanukkah. It lasts eight days and eight nights. Each night, his family lights a candle.

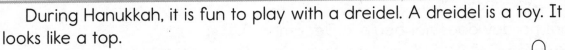

1. Whom is this story about?
    A. James   B. Micah
2. How many nights does Hanukkah last?
    A. one   B. eight
3. What does his family do each night?
    A. light a candle   B. shop

Day 2

During Hanukkah, it is fun to play with a dreidel. A dreidel is a toy. It looks like a top.

1. What is a **dreidel**?
    A. a toy   B. a food
2. Which word rhymes with **look**?
    A. hook   B. moon
3. What is the topic?
    A. fun   B. dreidels

Day 3

Andrew's family celebrates Kwanzaa. It lasts for a week. Each night, his family wears special clothes and lights a candle.

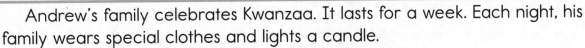

1. What does Andrew's family do during Kwanzaa?
    A. lights candles   B. blows out a candle
2. How long does Kwanzaa last?
    A. a night   B. a week
3. Andrew's family wears special _____.
    A. candles   B. clothes

Day 4

Holidays and Gifts

Many families celebrate a special holiday in December. Christmas, Hanukkah, and Kwanzaa all begin in December. Each holiday has special foods and traditions.

1. In which month does Christmas happen?
    A. March   B. December

2. What holiday does not begin in December?
    A. Kwanzaa   B. Valentine's Day

3. What do all of the holidays have?
    A. special foods   B. stockings

4. Draw a picture of a holiday that is special to you.

Apples and grapes are fruits. They are both sweet. Fruits are good snacks.

1. How does a grape taste?
   A. sweet   B. spicy
2. Apples are _____.
   A. vegetables   B. fruits
3. What is your favorite fruit?

_____

Milk and water are healthful drink choices. Sodas have a lot of sugar. They are not the best drink choice.

1. Which is the more healthful choice?
   A. milk   B. soda
2. What do sodas have in them?
   A. pepper   B. sugar
3. Which word is the opposite of **best**?
   A. good   B. worst

Foods from the dairy group are good for your bones. Milk, cheese, and yogurt are all in the dairy group.

1. Cheese is in which food group?   A. fruit   B. dairy
2. Say the name of each picture. Which word has the **long o** sound as in **bone**?

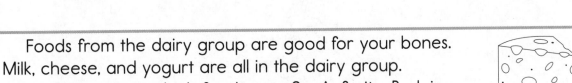

   A.   B.
3. What are two foods that are in the dairy group?

_____   _____

Grains include foods made from wheat, rice, and oats. Whole grains are the best choice. Whole wheat bread and brown rice are both whole grain foods.

1. Rice is a kind of _____.
   A. grain   B. fruit
2. Which is a whole grain food?

   A.   B.
3. Draw a picture of two whole grain foods.

Food and Nutrition

Jamie wants to eat a healthful lunch. She chooses one food from each food group. She has a salad with chicken, a glass of milk, pretzels, and an orange.

1. Which food group is chicken in?
   A. protein   B. fruit

2. Which is a part of the dairy group?

   A.   B.

3. When does the story take place?
   A. noon   B. nighttime

4. Draw a picture of what you would have for lunch.

Name_____

Day 1

In winter, bears sleep in dens. Some bears use a cave as their den. They stay in their dens for five to six months.

1. A **den** is where a bear _____.
   A. fishes   B. sleeps
2. In which season do bears sleep?
   A. winter   B. summer
3. Which word means the opposite of **stay**?
   A. leave   B. play

Day 2

Hedgehogs hibernate in winter. They eat insects, which are hard to find in winter. Hedgehogs hibernate to stay alive.

1. Which is another meaning of **sleep all winter**?
   A. hibernate   B. hunt
2. What do hedgehogs eat?
   A. bread   B. insects
3. Why do they hibernate?
   A. for fun   B. to stay alive

Day 3

Some animals go underground in winter. Snakes, alligators, and frogs go into a hole in the mud. They hibernate until warm weather returns.

1. Where do frogs live in winter?
   A. in the mud   B. in a pond
2. Draw a snake hibernating.

3. Say the name of each picture. Which word has the **long a** sound as in **snake**? A.   B.

Day 4

Brown bears eat a lot to get ready for winter. They eat fish, berries, grass, and roots. In autumn, they may eat up to 90 pounds of food a day.

1. How do bears get ready for winter?
   A. by eating a lot   B. by gathering nuts
2. What do bears eat?
   A.   B.
3. Draw a picture of how bears get ready for winter.

Hibernation

Many animals hibernate in the winter. Brown bears, groundhogs, and hedgehogs all hibernate. They rest during winter and become active in spring.

1. Which describes a bear in spring?
    A. bear sleeping in cave   B. thin bear eating grass

2. Which is an animal that hibernates?

    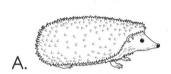   

    A.   B.

3. Underline the word or the phrase in the story that means the opposite of **resting**.

4. Draw a picture of an animal hibernating.

 K.RI.1, K.RI.2, K.RI.4, K.RI.7, K.RF.3, K.RF.4, K.W.2, K.W.3, K.L.4, K.L.5   CD-104595 • © Carson-Dellosa

Winter is Carter's favorite season. It comes after autumn and before spring. Carter loves the cold weather that happens in winter.

1. What is Carter's favorite season?
   A. autumn   B. winter
2. What is Carter's favorite thing about winter?
   A. warm weather   B. cold weather
3. Which word is the opposite of **before**?
   A. during   B. after

In winter, the trees are bare. All of the leaves are gone. It is too cold for new leaves to grow.

1. Which word describes a tree in winter?
   A. bare   B. full
2. What does the word **bare** mean in this story?
   A. an animal   B. empty
3. Why do leaves not grow in winter?
   A. too cold   B. too warm

Animals get ready for winter in different ways. Some animals migrate, or move where it is warm. Other animals hibernate in winter.

1. What does **migrate** mean?
   A. to move   B. to sleep
2. Where do animals migrate to?
   A. someplace warm   B. someplace cold
3. When do some animals hibernate?
   A. summer   B. winter

Kevin wears warm clothes in winter. Mittens keep his hands warm. A hat and scarf keep his head and neck warm.

1. Who is the main character?
   A. winter   B. Kevin
2. What does he wear to keep his head warm?
   A. mittens   B. a hat
3. Draw a picture of how Kevin might look in summer.

Winter

Winter is the season with the shortest days. It is also the season with the coldest weather. In many places, it will snow in winter.

1. Winter days are _____.
   A. long   B. short

2. Winter weather is _____ than other seasons.
   A. colder   B. warmer

3. Which is most likely happening on a winter day?
   A. kids swimming at a beach
   B. kids bundled up building a snowman

4. Draw a picture of your favorite thing that happens in winter.

Katy loves to play in the snow. She and her brother, Ryan, sled. They also build snow forts.

1. Who is Ryan?
   A. Katy's friend   B. Katy's brother
2. What do Katy and Ryan like to do in the snow?
   A. eat ice cream   B. sled
3. Which picture shows a **sled**?

   A.   B.

Day 1

Piper wants to build a snowman. She has a carrot for the nose. Her sister finds buttons and a hat. They work together to build a snowman.

1. What does Piper want to make?
   A. a snow fort   B. a snowman
2. Who helps Piper?
   A. her sister   B. her brother
3. Draw what the snowman will look like.

Day 2

Nick loves how snow looks and feels. Snow is white. Snow is soft and cold.

1. Which word tells how snow looks?
   A. cold   B. white
2. Which word tells how snow feels?
   A. white   B. soft
3. Which word is the opposite of **soft**?
   A. hard   B. fluffy

Day 3

Quan and Mark play sports in the snow. Quan likes to ski. Mark likes to snowboard.

1. What does Quan like to do?
   A. ski   B. snowboard
2. Which word begins with the **sk** sound as in **ski**?
   A. sweater   B. skate
3. What would you like to do in the snow?

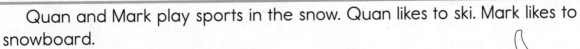

Day 4

The Snowmen

The boys and girls made snowmen. The boys worked together to build a snowman that had sticks for arms and a scarf around its neck. The girls made a snowman with a baseball cap and a coat. They were all happy with the two snowmen.

1. Who made a snowman with a cap and a coat?
   A. the boys   B. the girls

2. Who felt happy?
   A. the boys   B. the girls   C. both the boys and the girls

3. Draw a picture of the girls' snowman.

4. Tell a friend one thing that is the same about each snowman and one thing that is different.

 K.RL.1, K.RL.3, K.RL.4, K.RL.7, K.RF.2, K.RF.3, K.RF.4, K.W.1, K.W.3, K.L.5   CD-104595 • © Carson-Dellosa

Day 1

Penguins are birds that do not fly. They have flippers that help them swim. They spend time in water and on land.

1. Penguins are a kind of _____.
   A. bird   B. fish
2. What helps penguins swim?
   A. their flippers   B. their beaks
3. Where do penguins live?
   A. on land   B. in water   C. both land and water

Day 2

There are many kinds of penguins. They live in different places. No penguins live at the North Pole.

1. What word means the same as **kinds** as used in the story?
   A. types   B. nice
2. Where do penguins live?
   A. different places   B. North Pole
3. Where do penguins **not** live?
   A. North Pole   B. South Pole

Day 3

Chinstrap penguins are Rob's favorite. They have a black band under their heads. They eat fish.

1. Who likes Chinstrap penguins?
   A. Rob   B. Ray
2. What color is the band under their heads?
   A. red   B. black
3. Which picture shows what penguins eat?

   A.   B.

Day 4

Penguins lay eggs. Some penguins make nests. Other penguins use their feet to care for the eggs.

1. What do some penguins use to take care of the eggs?
   A. their feet   B. their flippers
2. Underline one word in the story that has a **long a** sound.
3. Which means more than one?
   A. egg   B. eggs

Emperor Penguins

Emperor penguins are the largest of all penguins. They live on the ice. They huddle together to stay warm.

1. Emperor penguins are _____.
   A. large   B. small

2. Where do they live?
   A. on the ice   B. in the desert

3. Say the name of each picture. Which word has the **long i** sound as in **ice**?

   A.

                               B.

4. Write one way you stay warm when you are cold. _____

   _____

Name_____

Some brown bears are called grizzly bears. They can be up to seven feet tall. Some weigh as much as 700 pounds.

1. What is another name for some brown bears?
   A. teddy bears   B. grizzly bears
2. How tall can brown bears be?
   A. 700 pounds   B. 7 feet tall
3. Which word sounds the same as **weigh** but is spelled differently?
   A. way   B. measure

Baby bears are called cubs. Cubs are born in winter. They live off their mother's milk for a year.

1. What is a baby bear called?
   A. cute   B. a cub
2. When are cubs born?
   A. summer   B. winter
3. Say the name of each picture. Which word rhymes with **born**?

   A.   B.

Polar bears live in the cold. They have fat that helps them stay warm. They have black skin and clear fur.

1. Which animal lives in the cold?
   A. a panda   B. a polar bear
2. Fat helps polar bears stay _____.
   A. full   B. warm
3. Write one fact about polar bears. _____

   _____

Polar bears are wild animals. They hunt for food. Seals are the main part of a polar bear's diet.

1. Polar bears are _____.
   A. tame   B. wild
2. How do polar bears get their food?
   A. they hunt   B. they shop
3. **Diet** tells what an animal _____.
   A. eats   B. sees

Pandas

Pandas have black and white fur. They are good at climbing trees. They eat bamboo.

1. Which animal has black and white fur?
    A. a polar bear   B. a panda

2. What do pandas eat?
    A. fish   B. bamboo

3. Which picture shows the word **climb**?

    A.   B.

4. Which word is the opposite of **good**?
    A. well   B. bad

Name_____

There are many kinds of transportation. Some, such as airplanes, move in the air. Trains, cars, and buses move on land. Others travel on water.

1. Which moves in air?
   A. a train   B. an airplane
2. How do you travel home from school? _____

3. What travels in water? _____

Day 1

Carlos has a long way to travel. He will fly on an airplane. The airplane can go much faster than a car.

1. Which is faster?
   A. an airplane   B. a car
2. Which word describes the distance Carlos will travel?
   A. near   B. far
3. Which word is more than one?
   A. car   B. cars

Day 2

Claire has four kinds of transportation. She has a bike, roller skates, and a car. She also gets to places by walking.

1. Which does Claire not have?
   A. a car   B. a boat
2. How many kinds of transportation does Claire have?
   A. three   B. four
3. Draw one way Claire can travel from one place to another.

Day 3

Boats can carry people across water. Ferries can carry both cars and people across water. Both boats and ferries are types of water transportation.

1. Boats carry people across _____.
   A. land   B. water
2. Which can move a car across water?
   A. a boat   B. a ferry
3. What is the same about boats and ferries?
   A. both move on water   B. they are the same size

Day 4

Getting to School

Students in Ms. Smith's class came to school in different ways. Ten students rode the school bus. Six came in a car. Two students walked to school.

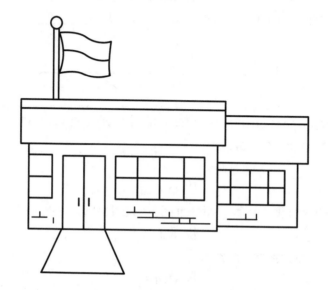

1. How many students walk to school?
    A. two   B. ten

2. How do most of the students get to school?
    A. by car   B. by school bus

3. Where are all of the students going?
    A. to school   B. to the park

4. Which word is the opposite of **different**?
    A. same   B. done

Groundhog Day is February 2. If the groundhog sees his shadow, it is said we will have six more weeks of winter. If he does not, it is said we will have an early spring.

1. In which month is Groundhog Day?   A. July   B. February
2. Draw a picture of what the groundhog looks like if we are going to have an early spring.

3. Say the name of each picture. Which word has the **short i** sound as in **six**?   A.   B.

Day 1

Groundhogs eat a lot in summer. When cold weather comes, they burrow underground. They do not come out again until spring.

1. When do groundhogs eat a lot?
   A. winter   B. summer
2. When do groundhogs come out from underground?
   A. spring   B. autumn
3. Which words describe **burrow**?
   A. under the ground   B. above the ground

Day 2

Groundhogs are in the squirrel family. They can climb trees. They are also able to swim.

1. What family are groundhogs in?   A.   B.
2. What can both squirrels and groundhogs do?
   A. climb trees   B. fly
3. Say the name of each picture. Which word begins with the **sw** sound as in **swim**?
   A.   B.

Day 3

Groundhogs are also called whistle-pigs. When in danger, they make a loud whistling sound. This sound tells other groundhogs of the danger.

1. What is another name for groundhogs?
   A. whistle-pigs   B. horn hogs
2. What sound do they make when in danger?
   A. a whistle   B. an oink
3. Which word means the same as **loud**?
   A. noisy   B. quiet

Day 4

Groundhog Day

The groundhog popped up from his hole. It was a sunny day. He saw his shadow. People believe there will be six more weeks of winter.

1. What was the weather like in the story?
    A. sunny   B. cloudy

2. What did the groundhog see?
    A. people   B. his shadow

3. How many more weeks of winter will there be?
    A. six   B. two

4. Draw what the weather might be on a day the groundhog does not see his shadow.

Name_____

Addy gave her mom a card. It had a big heart on it. She colored the heart pink.

1. Whom did Addy give a card to?
   A. her mom   B. her dad
2. What was on the card?
   A. flower   B. heart
3. Draw a picture of a card you will make for someone.

Day 1

Some people give gifts on Valentine's Day. A card can be a gift. Flowers and candy are also kinds of gifts.

1. What is another word for **gift**?
   A. present   B. happy
2. Say the name of each picture. Which word has the **ar** sound as in **card**?

   A.
   B.
3. Which word is more than one?   A. flower   B. flowers

Day 2

Paul's class will share valentines. He made one for each student. Paul made a special valentine for his teacher.

1. Whose class is sharing valentines?
   A. Paul's   B. Val's
2. Whom did he make a special card for?
   A. his friend   B. his teacher
3. Which word has the **long a** sound as in **made**?
   A. cane   B. can

Day 3

Jayla wanted to send a valentine to her nana. She made a card. Her mom helped her mail it. Nana loved it.

1. Whom did Jayla send a card to?
   A. her mom   B. her nana
2. Who helped Jayla?
   A. her mom   B. her nana
3. Draw how Nana might have looked when she read the card.

Day 4

Valentine's Day

Mr. Jones read special books to his class about Valentine's Day. Look at the books to see what he read.

1. Which book has a question in the title?
   A. *Polly the Pup Sends a Valentine*   B. *What Is Valentine's Day?*

2. Which book will most likely tell you more about the holiday?
   A. *Mom's Secret Valentine*   B. *What Is Valentine's Day?*

3. Which book is fiction?
   A. *What Is Valentine's Day?*   B. *Polly the Pup Sends a Valentine*

4. Which book would you most like to read? Write two sentences. _____

   _____

   _____

   _____

Skin covers the body. It holds the body together. We use our skin to touch.

1. Skin covers our _____.
   A. hair   B. bodies

2. Say the name of each picture. Which word rhymes with **skin**?

   A.   B.

3. Skin lets us _____.
   A. touch   B. smell

The heart is a muscle. It pumps blood. The heart is the size of a fist.

1. The heart pumps _____.
   A. muscles   B. blood

2. The heart is the same size as a _____.
   A. fist   B. basketball

3. Say the name of each picture. Which word begins with the **bl** sound as in **blood**?

   A.   B.

The body has more than 200 bones. The biggest bone is in the leg. The smallest bone is in the ear.

1. The biggest bone is in the _____.
   A. ear   B. leg

2. The smallest bone is in the _____.
   A. ear   B. leg

3. The body has _____ 200 bones.
   A. more than   B. less than

The body has many parts. The head has eyes, ears, a nose, and a mouth. The head is at the top of the body.

1. Which word is the opposite of **top**?
   A. head   B. bottom

2. What is on the head?
   A. eyes   B. fingers

3. Say the name of each picture. Which word rhymes with **nose**?

   A.   B.

Taking Care of Your Body

Rosa takes care of her body. She eats healthful foods. She takes a bath at night. She brushes her teeth two times a day. Rosa puts sunscreen on her skin. She runs to keep her heart strong. She also gets lots of sleep.

1. How does Rosa care for her heart?
   A. she puts on sunscreen   B. she runs

2. Which word means the same as **rest**?
   A. sleep   B. run

3. Which is not a way Rosa cares for her body?
   A. brushing her teeth   B. eating ice cream

4. Draw a picture of one way you take care of your body.

 K.RL.1, K.RL.3, K.RL.4, K.RI.1, K.RI.2, K.RI.4, K.RF.2, K.RF.4, K.W.1, K.W.8, K.L.4, K.L.5   CD-104595 • © Carson-Dellosa

The dentist helps take care of your teeth. You should see the dentist two times a year. The dentist looks at your teeth. She makes sure your teeth are clean and healthy.

1. The dentist takes care of _____.
   A. ears   B. teeth
2. How many times a year should you see the dentist?
   A. one   B. two
3. Which word has the **long e** sound as in **teeth**?
   A. feet   B. hen

Day 1

Ivy brushes her teeth. She uses toothpaste. She puts toothpaste on her toothbrush.

1. Ivy uses toothpaste to brush her _____.
   A. hair   B. teeth
2. Which word is a compound word like **toothbrush**?
   A. football   B. teeth
3. Whom is this story about?
   A. Ivy   B. Meg

Day 2

Too much sugar is bad for your teeth. It can cause a cavity. A cavity is a hole in the tooth.

1. Sugar can cause a _____.
   A. tooth   B. cavity
2. Draw a picture of a tooth with a cavity.

3. Which word ends with the same **th** sound as in **tooth**?
   A. tent   B. path

Day 3

Zara brushes her teeth two times a day. She also uses floss to clean between her teeth. She likes to take care of her teeth.

1. How many times a day does Zara brush her teeth?
   A. one   B. two
2. What is another way she takes care of her teeth?
   A. she uses floss   B. she uses mouthwash
3. Floss cleans _____ teeth.
   A. under   B. between

Day 4

A Visit with the Dentist

Owen has a toothache. He goes to the dentist. The dentist helps Owen's sick tooth. His tooth doesn't hurt anymore.

1. What part of Owen hurts?
    A. his foot   B. his tooth

2. Who helps Owen feel better?
    A. dentist   B. mom

3. **Doesn't** is the contraction for which two words?
    A. do not   B. does not

4. Which tooth does the dentist help?
    A. the well tooth   B. the sick tooth

One of the five senses is sight. We use our eyes to see. Some people wear glasses to see better.

1. Sight is one of the five _____.
   A. eyes   B. senses
2. What tool can help some people see better?
   A. glasses   B. gloves
3. Which word is more than one?
   A. eye   B. eyes

We smell with our noses. We can smell sweet things, like flowers. Our noses also smell rotten things, like garbage.

1. What sense do we use our noses for?
   A. touching   B. smelling
2. Which food smells sweet?
   A. eggs   B. fruit

3. What do you like to smell? _____

Rex uses his tongue to taste food. He likes the taste of sweet things. Ice cream is his favorite.

1. What does Rex use to taste food?
   A. his eyes   B. his tongue
2. What does he like the taste of?
   A. ice cream   B. pickles
3. What do you not like the taste of?

_____

We use our ears to hear. Some people have a hard time hearing. They may wear hearing aids to help them.

1. What do we use to hear?
   A. the nose   B. the ears
2. Hearing aids can help some people hear _____.
   A. worse   B. better
3. What is the topic?
   A. smell   B. hearing

The Five Senses

Our five senses are sight, touch, taste, smell, and hearing. Different parts of our bodies help with each sense. Eyes help us see. Hands and skin help us feel and touch. Tongues tell us how something tastes. Our ears help us hear, and our noses let us smell.

1. How many senses are there?
   A. four   B. five

2. What part of the body helps us smell?
   A. the hand   B. the nose

3. To taste, we use our _____.
   A. ears   B. tongues

4. What is your favorite sense? _____

Kites need wind to fly. The longer the string, the higher the kite can fly.

1. Wind helps kites _____.
   A. fly   B. rest
2. Which word is the opposite of **long**?
   A. high   B. short
3. Which word is more than one?
   A. kite   B. kites

Bella's kite is blue. It has a red tail. Bella loves her kite.

1. Who has a kite?
   A. Ben   B. Bella
2. What color is the kite's tail?
   A. red   B. blue
3. Say the name of each picture. Which word has the **long i** sound as in **kite**?

   A.   B.

Pedro flies his kite at the park. He has space to run. He goes every Sunday to fly his kite.

1. Where does Pedro fly his kite?
   A. in his yard   B. at the park
2. When does he go?
   A. every day   B. every Sunday
3. Say the name of each picture. Which word rhymes with **run**?

   A.   B.

Ellie's kite is in a tree. Her dad helps get it down. She is happy to have her kite back.

1. Where is Ellie's kite?
   A. in the sky   B. in a tree

2. Which word in the story is the opposite of **up**? _____
3. Draw what happens after the kite is in a tree.

Flying Kites

Tony and his sister, Gina, each have a kite. Tony's kite is green. It has a car on it. Gina's kite is blue. Her kite has a cat on it. They both love to fly their kites.

1. Who is Tony's sister?   A. Tina   B. Gina

2. Who has a green kite?   A. Tony   B. Gina

3. Who has a kite with a cat on it?   A. Tony   B. Gina

4. How are Tony and Gina alike? Write a sentence. _____

_____

The leprechaun is little. He has red hair. He is wearing a black hat.

1. The leprechaun is _____.
   A. big   B. little
2. What color is the hat?
   A. red   B. black
3. Which word means the same as **little**?
   A. big   B. small

Kelly wears green on St. Patrick's Day. She is wearing a green dress and green socks. Green is her favorite color.

1. Whom is this story about?
   A. Patrick   B. Kelly
2. What is Kelly wearing?
   A. brown socks   B. a green dress
3. Which word is more than one?
   A. dress   B. dresses

The shamrock is green. It has three leaves. A shamrock is also called a clover.

1. How many leaves does a shamrock have?
   A. three   B. two
2. Another name for shamrock is _____.
   A. clover   B. lucky

3. Which picture shows a **shamrock**?   A.   B.

The leprechaun has a pot of gold. The pot is black. The gold coins are heavy and shiny.

1. What is in the pot?
   A. gold   B. black
2. What color is the pot?
   A. gold   B. black
3. Which word has the **oi** sound as in **coin**?
   A. point   B. cow

The Four-Leaf Clover

Aiden finds a four-leaf clover. He feels lucky. He shows the clover to his mom. She is very happy for Aiden.

1. What did Aiden find?
   A. leaves   B. a clover

2. Who feels lucky?
   A. Aiden   B. Aiden's mom

3. Say the name of each picture. Which word begins with the **sh** sound as in **show**?

    A.   B.

4. Whom does Aiden show the clover to?
   A. his dad   B. his mom

 K.RL.1, K.RL.3, K.RL.4, K.RL.7, K.RI.1, K.RI.2, K.RI.4, K.RI.7, K.RF.2, K.RF.3, K.RF.4, K.L.1, K.L.4   CD-104595 • © Carson-Dellosa

It rained all morning. The rain stopped, and the sun came out. A beautiful rainbow was in the sky.

1. When did it rain?
   A. all day   B. all morning
2. Say the name of each picture. Which word has the **short u** sound as in **sun**?
   A.   B.
3. Draw what happened after it stopped raining.

Lila loves rainbows. Her favorite color of the rainbow is red. She has a sweater with a rainbow on it.

1. What does Lila like?
   A. sweaters   B. rainbows
2. What is her favorite color?
   A. green   B. red
3. What is your favorite color of the rainbow?
   _____

Molly made a rainbow. She used colored paper. She had red, orange, yellow, green, blue, and purple paper.

1. What did Molly use to make a rainbow?
   A. paper   B. crayons
2. Which color did she not use?
   A. orange   B. brown
3. How many colors did she use?
   A. five   B. six

The rainbow is colorful. It is in the sky. The rainbow has puffy white clouds beside it.

1. The clouds are _____ the rainbow.
   A. under   B. beside
2. Which word means the same as **puffy**?
   A. fluffy   B. flat
3. Underline the color word in the story.

Rainbows

Harper read two books about rainbows. One book was the story of a leprechaun who lived at the end of a rainbow. The other book told about how rainbows are made. Harper liked both books.

1. How many books did Harper read?
   A. one   B. two

2. Which book is fiction?
   A. *Lucky's Rainbow*   B. *All About Rainbows*

3. Which book tells facts about rainbows?
   A. *Lucky's Rainbow*   B. *All About Rainbows*

4. Which book would you like to read? Tell a friend why.

Clouds are made of water. Rain falls from clouds.
1. What are clouds made of?
    A. cotton   B. water
2. Say the name of each picture. Which word has the same number of syllables as **water**?
    A.   B.
3. What do you like to do when it rains? Write a sentence. _____

_____

Day 1

Ty likes to watch clouds. He likes white, puffy clouds. They look like cotton.
1. What color are the clouds Ty likes?   A. gray   B. white
2. What is one way clouds and cotton are alike?

_____

3. What is one way clouds and cotton are different?

_____

Day 2

Fog is a kind of cloud. It is close to the ground. Fog can be hard to see through.
1. Fog is a kind of _____.
    A. ground   B. cloud
2. Which word means the same as **close**?
    A. far   B. near
3. Tell a friend why fog is hard to see through.

Day 3

Some clouds are white. Some are dark. Dark clouds can mean a storm is coming.
1. What is the topic?   A. storms   B. clouds
2. Dark clouds could mean a _____ is coming.
    A. storm   B. sun
3. Say the name of each picture. Which word has the **ar** sound as in **dark**?
    A.    B.

Day 4

Cloud Watching

A.J. and his dad like to watch clouds. They lie on the grass and look at the sky. A.J. sees a cloud that looks like a ship. His dad sees a cloud that looks like an airplane. They both see the cloud that looks like a cat.

1. Who sees a cloud that looks like an airplane?
   A. A.J.   B. his dad

2. Which word begins with the **sh** sound as in **ship**?
   A. sheep   B. snow

3. What is the setting of the story?
   A. inside   B. outside

4. How are A.J. and his dad alike?
   A. They both like sports.   B. They both like watching clouds.

 K.RL.1, K.RL.3, K.RI.1, K.RI.2, K.RI.3, K.RI.4, K.RF.2, K.RF.3, K.RF.4, K.W.1, K.W.2, K.L.4   CD-104595 • © Carson-Dellosa

Stella wants to go swimming. She puts on her pink swimsuit. She wears sandals and a purple hat.

1. What does Stella want to do?
   A. build a sandcastle   B. swim
2. Sandals and a hat are both kinds of _____.
   A. toys   B. clothes
3. What color is her swimsuit?
   A. purple   B. pink

Day 1

Cam wants to play in the snow. He puts on a coat and hat. He wears his blue gloves and red scarf.

1. Where does Cam want to play?
   A. inside   B. outside
2. Say the name of each picture. Which word has the **long o** sound as in **coat**?

   A.   B.
3. Draw a picture whose name rhymes with **hat**.

Day 2

Paula has clothes for rainy days. She has a yellow raincoat. She also has purple rain boots that keep her feet dry.

1. What helps keep Paula's feet dry?
   A. raincoat   B. rain boots
2. Which other item might Paula need on a rainy day?
   A. an umbrella   B. sunglasses
3. Which word is the opposite of **dry**?
   A. cold   B. wet

Day 3

At bedtime, Silas wears pajamas. His pajamas have trains on them. His pajama top has six buttons on it.

1. When does Silas wear pajamas?
   A. at lunchtime   B. at bedtime
2. Say the name of each picture. Which word begins with the **tr** sound as in **train**?

   A.   B.
3. Draw one thing you do to get ready for bed.

Day 4

Kate's Clothes

Kate takes care of her clothes. She puts her dirty clothes in the basket. When the basket is full, she washes the clothes. After the clothes are clean, she puts them in the dryer. When the clothes are dry, she folds them and puts them away.

1. Which is one way Kate takes care of her clothes?
   A. she folds them   B. she buys them

2. Where does she put dirty clothes?
   A. a dresser   B. a laundry basket

3. Say the name of each picture. Which word begins with the **f** sound as in **fold**?

   A.   B.

4. Draw a picture to show the steps Kate takes to care for her clothes.

Kyle likes the rain. He wears rain boots and a raincoat. He likes to jump in puddles.
1. What does Kyle wear?
   A. raincoat   B. swimsuit
2. What is the setting?
   A. inside   B. outside
3. What do rain and snow have in common? Write a sentence. _____

_____

It is snowing. The snow is white. It is cold.
1. Which word names a color?
   A. cold   B. white
2. Which word is the opposite of **cold**?
   A. hot   B. hold
3. Draw one thing you would wear in the snow.

It is sunny. The sun is hot. Jack wears sunglasses.
1. What is the weather?
   A. cloudy   B. sunny
2. What does he wear?
   A. cap   B. sunglasses
3. Draw a picture of what you would wear on a sunny day.

When air moves, it is called wind. A gentle wind is called a breeze. A strong wind is a gust.
1. A gust is a _____ wind.
   A. gentle   B. strong
2. A gentle wind is a _____.
   A. breeze   B. gust
3. What else is gentle?

_____

The Storm

Last night, a storm passed over Lori's town. The lightning was bright. The thunder was loud. Wind blew leaves off trees. It rained all night.

1. When was the storm?
   A. this morning   B. last night

2. What blew the leaves?
   A. wind   B. rain

3. Which word rhymes with **bright**?
   A. night   B. brim

4. Draw two things that happened during the storm.

Name_____

People live on Earth. Earth is a planet. It is our home.
1. Earth is a _____.
   A. plant   B. planet
2. Which word ends with the same **th** sound as in **Earth**?
   A. tooth   B. thumb
3. Earth is our _____.
   A. home   B. friend

Tia takes care of our Earth. She turns off the lights. Tia is saving energy.
1. What does Tia take care of?
   A. lights   B. Earth
2. Which word is the opposite of **off**?
   A. down   B. on
3. Draw a picture of another way Tia can save energy.

Andy takes bags to the store with him. He does not use the store's bags. He saves paper by bringing his own bags.
1. What does Andy take to the store?
   A. paper   B. bags
2. Say the name of each picture. Which word rhymes with **bring**?
   A.   B.
3. What is Andy saving by bringing his own bags?
   A. stores   B. paper

Lucy does not waste water. When she brushes her teeth, she turns off the water. She only turns the water on when she needs it.
1. What is Lucy doing in the story?
   A. taking a bath   B. brushing her teeth
2. What is Lucy saving?
   A. paper   B. water
3. Which word is the opposite of **waste**?
   A. save   B. use

Recycling

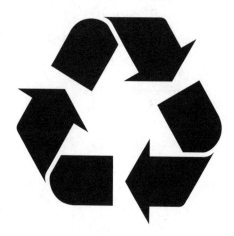

Recycling helps the earth. Paper, plastic, some metals, and glass can all be recycled. Maria and Jill collect things to recycle. Maria finds soda cans, newspapers, and empty jars. Jill finds water bottles and magazines.

1. What are Maria and Jill doing?
   A. playing   B. recycling

2. Who finds newspapers?
   A. Maria   B. Jill

3. Which is not able to be recycled?
   A. an apple core   B. a water bottle

4. Draw a picture of the things Maria and Jill find.

Butterflies are insects. They have four wings. They can fly.
1. What is the topic of the story?
   A. wings   B. butterflies
2. How many wings does a butterfly have?
   A. two   B. four
3. Draw a picture of another animal that has wings and can fly.

Day 1

Butterflies lay eggs. They lay their eggs on leaves. Caterpillars hatch from the eggs.
1. Which is another word for **hatch**?
   A. hide   B. born
2. Which word has the **long e** sound as in **leaf**?
   A. bean   B. bed
3. What is a baby butterfly called?
   A. a fly baby   B. a caterpillar

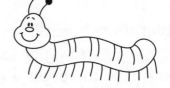

Day 2

The caterpillar is green. It hatched from an egg. The caterpillar eats leaves.
1. What color is the caterpillar?
   A. white   B. green

2. What do caterpillars eat? _____
3. Draw a picture of another animal that hatches from an egg.

Day 3

Quincy has a butterfly garden. The garden is filled with flowers. The butterflies like to drink from the flowers.
1. Who likes the flowers?
   A. dogs   B. butterflies
2. Butterflies _____ from the flowers.
   A. drink   B. sit
3. What is the setting of the story?
   A. a butterfly garden   B. a cave

Day 4

The Butterfly Life Cycle

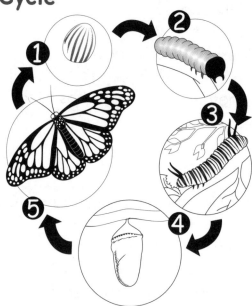

Caterpillars hatch from eggs. They eat leaves. When a caterpillar is grown, it will hang from a twig or leaf in a sack. It is called a pupa. A beautiful butterfly comes out of the pupa. The butterfly lays an egg on a leaf.

1. Which picture shows a pupa?

   A.
   B.

2. What comes after the pupa?

   A.
   B.

3. Which lays eggs?

   A.
   B.

4. What comes between egg and pupa?

   A.
   B.

 K.RL.1, K.RL.3, K.RI.1, K.RI.2, K.RI.3, K.RI.4, K.RI.7, K.RF.3, K.RF.4, K.W.8, K.L.4 CD-104595 • © Carson-Dellosa

The frog is green. It eats bugs. It lives in the pond.

1. What does the frog eat?
   A. apples   B. bugs
2. Where does the frog live?
   A. in the woods   B. in the pond
3. Say the name of each picture. Which word begins with the **fr** sound as in **frog**?

   A.   B.

Day 1

Frogs lay eggs. The eggs are in water. Baby frogs are called tadpoles.

1. The topic of the story is turtles.
   A. true   B. false
2. Do frogs lay eggs?
   A. yes   B. no
3. What are baby frogs called?
   A. tadpoles   B. fish

Day 2

Tadpoles look like fish. They have long tails. They breathe through gills.

1. What helps tadpoles breathe?
   A. the gills   B. the tail
2. Which word is the opposite of **long**?
   A. thin   B. short
3. Tell a friend one way a tadpole and a fish are the same.

Day 3

Whitney has a pet frog. His name is Jumpy. Jumpy has strong legs that help him jump high.

1. Who has a pet?
   A. Jumpy   B. Whitney

2. What is the pet's name? _____
3. Which word is the opposite of **strong**?
   A. hard   B. weak

Day 4

The Red-Eyed Tree Frog

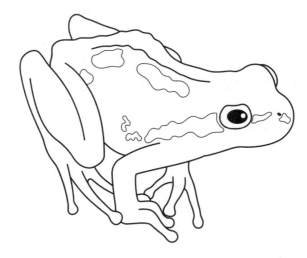

The red-eyed tree frog lives in the rain forest. It rests during the day. It is active at night. It eats bugs and flies.

1. What is the topic?
    A. the rain forest   B. the red-eyed tree frog

2. When does it rest?
    A. during the day   B. at night

3. What does it eat?
    A. strawberries   B. flies

4. How are the red-eyed tree frog and a common frog the same? Write a sentence.

    _____

    _____

 K.RL.1, K.RL.3, K.RL.4, K.RI.1, K.RI.2, K.RI.3, K.RI.4, K.RF.2, K.RF.4, K.W.2, K.L.5   CD-104595 • © Carson-Dellosa

Cows live on the farm. The cows are black with white spots. The farmer milks the cow.

1. What color are the cows' spots?   A. black   B. white
2. Who takes care of the cows?
   A. a farmer   B. a police officer
3. Say the name of each picture. Which word begins with the **sp** sound as in **spot**?

   A.
                           B.

This farm has ducks. The ducks swim in the pond. Mother ducks lay eggs.

1. What is the setting?
   A. the city   B. the farm
2. Say the name of each picture. Which word rhymes with **duck**?

   A.
                           B.
3. Draw one thing ducks do on the farm.

The brown horse has a saddle. The farmer rides the horse. The horse helps the farmer do his work.

1. What color is the horse?
   A. black   B. brown
2. The farmer _____ the horse.
   A. walks   B. rides
3. Draw one way the horse may help the farmer.

A mother chicken is called a hen. Hens lay eggs. Baby chickens are called chicks.

1. A baby chicken is called a _____.
   A. hen   B. chick
2. Both hens and chicks are _____.
   A. cows   B. chickens
3. Which lays eggs?
   A. hen   B. chick

Farm Animals

Chickens, cows, sheep, and horses are farm animals. They each make their own sounds. Some farm animals give us food. Cows make milk. Chickens give us eggs.

1. Which is not a farm animal?

A.

B.

2. Farm animals make the same sounds.   A. true   B. false

3. Which food comes from an animal?   A. eggs   B. bread

4. Draw a line from each animal to the food that she makes.

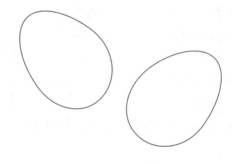

 K.RL.1, K.RL.3, K.RI.1, K.RI.2, K.RI.3, K.RF.2, K.RF.4, K.W.3, K.W.8   CD-104595 • © Carson-Dellosa

Cooper makes a card for his mom. He writes a poem inside the card. He gives his mom a hug and the card.

1. What does Cooper give his mom?

   A. flowers   B. a card

2. What did Cooper write?

   A. a list   B. a poem

3. Say the name of each picture. Which word has the **short u** sound as in **hug**?

   A.   B.

Jay's mom loves flowers. Jay buys his mom yellow flowers. She puts the flowers in a green vase.

1. Who loves flowers?

   A. Jay   B. Jay's mom

2. What color are the flowers?

   A. yellow   B. red

3. Where does Jay's mom put the flowers?

   A. in a vase   B. in a flowerpot

Kira makes her dad a special breakfast. She makes pancakes and a fruit cup. She pours a glass of orange juice. Her dad loves the breakfast.

1. What does Kira make?

   A. pancakes   B. toast

2. How do you think her dad feels?

   A. sad   B. happy

3. Draw a picture of what you like to eat for breakfast.

Heather and her mom go shopping. They look for a special gift for Dad. They buy a tie with a heart on it.

1. Whom does Heather go shopping with?

   A. her dad   B. her mom

2. Whom is she shopping for?

   A. her dad   B. her mom

3. What does Heather buy?

   A. a card   B. a tie

A Card for Mom

Grace bought her mom a card. It is pink and has flowers on it. Grace liked the poem on the front.

M — Mom, who loves me so
O — Offers me hugs
M — Means the world to me

1. What does Grace give her mom?
   A. flowers   B. a card

2. Circle the poem.

3. Which word is the opposite of **front**?
   A. side   B. back

4. Draw a picture of the card Grace bought for her mom.

K.RL.1, K.RL.3, K.RL.4, K.RL.5, K.RF.3, K.RF.4, K.W.1, K.W.3, K.L.5

Plants grow from seeds. They need water to grow. Plants also need sunshine.

1. What do plants grow from?
    A. water   B. seeds
2. Say the name of each picture. Which word has the **long e** sound as in **seed**?
    A.   B.
3. Tell two things plants need to grow.

Flowers are a part of plants. They have petals. Flowers also have stems.

1. Flowers are a part of _____.
    A. plants   B. roses
2. What is one thing flowers do not have?
    A. stems   B. faces
3. Draw a picture of a flower. Label two parts of the flower.

Theo and his mom plant a garden. They plant carrots, corn, and strawberries. The corn grows tall. The carrots grow underground.

1. What is the topic?
    A. the kitchen   B. the garden
2. What do they not plant?
    A. corn   B. apples
3. Which word is more than one?
    A. strawberry   B. strawberries

Nancy digs three small holes. She puts a seed in each hole. She puts dirt on top of the seeds.

1. Which word means the same as **dirt**?
    A. soil   B. snow
2. How many holes did Nancy dig?
    A. two   B. three
3. What goes in each hole?
    A. a seed   B. a plant

Parts of a Plant

Plants have many parts. The roots are underground. They help the plants get water from the dirt. Plants also have stems and leaves. Some plants grow flowers.

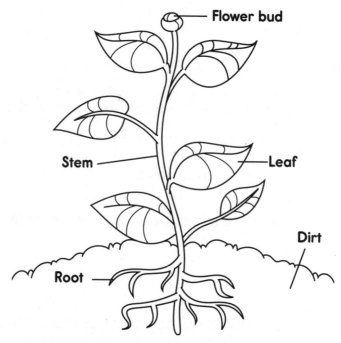

1. Which part of the plant is underground?
    A. the leaf   B. the root

2. Some _____ grow flowers.
    A. plants   B. roots

3. Which word is more than one?
    A. plant   B. plants

4. How many plants do you have in your home? _____
    Draw a picture of one.

 K.RL.1, K.RL.3, K.RL.4, K.RI.1, K.RI.2, K.RI.4, K.RI.7, K.RF.3, K.RF.4, K.W.2, K.W.3, K.W.8, K.L.1 CD-104595 • © Carson-Dellosa

Name_____

Sharks have fins. They have sharp teeth. Sharks eat fish.
1. Sharks eat _____.
    A. leaves   B. fish
2. Sharks have _____ teeth.
    A. dull   B. sharp
3. Say the name of each picture. Which word begins with the **f** sound as in **fin**?

    A. [feather]   B. [safety pin]

Day 1

An octopus has eight legs. It has no bones. An octopus can fit in small spaces.
1. What is the topic?
    A. an octopus   B. bones
2. How many legs does an octopus have?
    A. two   B. eight
3. Tell a friend one thing about an octopus.

Day 2

Many kinds of fish live in the ocean. They are all different colors. Some are very small, and others are very large.
1. Fish live _____ the ocean.
    A. in   B. on
2. Say the name of each picture. Which word has the **short i** sound as in **fish**?

    A. [bat]   B. [lips]
3. Draw your favorite ocean animal.

Day 3

A dolphin looks like a fish. It is not a fish. It breathes air through a hole on the top of its head.
1. A dolphin looks like a _____.
    A. fan   B. fish
2. Is a dolphin a fish?
    A. yes   B. no
3. What does a dolphin use to breathe?
    A. a hole on its head   B. its mouth

Day 4

85

Sea Turtles

Sea turtles live in the ocean. Female turtles lay eggs on the beach. When baby turtles hatch, they return to the ocean.

1. What is the topic?
   A. the ocean   B. sea turtles

2. Which cannot **hatch**?

   A.   B.

3. Sea turtles lay their eggs _____.
   A. on the beach   B. in the water

4. Tell a friend one fact about sea turtles.

Tamara goes to camp in the summer. She likes to make new friends. She sleeps in a tent.

1. Whom is the story about?
   A. Tamara   B. friends
2. What is the setting?
   A. school   B. camp
3. Write one thing Tamara does at camp.

_____

Day 1

Nassim and his family go to the beach. Nassim likes to build sand castles. His brother likes to find shells.

1. Where does Nassim go?
   A. the beach   B. the mountains
2. Who likes to find shells?
   A. Nassim   B. Nassim's brother
3. Draw a picture of what you like to do at the beach.

Day 2

Becca takes swim lessons. Her teacher is a lifeguard. Becca likes to swim underwater.

1. Whom is this story about?
   A. Becca   B. her teacher
2. What is she learning to do?
   A. play tennis   B. swim
3. Which word is the opposite of **take**?
   A. give   B. go

Day 3

Jacob likes to play sports in summer. He plays baseball with his friends. He plays tennis with his dad.

1. What does Jacob do in summer?
   A. sleep   B. play sports
2. What does Jacob play with his dad?
   A. baseball   B. tennis
3. What does Jacob play with his friends?
   A. baseball   B. tennis

Day 4

Peter's Summer

Peter loves summer. Every morning, he sleeps in. He spends the day at the pool. He swims with his friends. On the weekend, his family goes camping. They fish in the lake. They build a fire and roast marshmallows.

1. How does Peter spend his day?
   A. swimming   B. sleeping

2. Peter fishes _____ the lake.
   A. in   B. under

3. Whom does Peter camp with?
   A. his friends   B. his family

4. Draw a picture of two things Peter does when camping.

K.RL.1, K.RL.3, K.RL.4, K.RL.7, K.RF.4, K.W.2, K.W.3, K.W.8, K.L.1, K.L.5

Answer Key

Page 9
Day 1: 1. B; 2. A; 3. B;
Day 2: 1. B; 2. B; 3. A;
Day 3: 1. B; 2. A; 3. Answers will vary;
Day 4: 1. B; 2. A; 3. A

Page 10
1. A; 2. A; 3. A; 4. A

Page 11
Day 1: 1. A; 2. Check students' drawings;
3. Answers will vary;
Day 2: 1. B; 2. B; 3. It has
a loud siren.;
Day 3: 1. A; 2. Answers will vary; 3. A;
Day 4: 1. B; 2. A; 3. B

Page 12
1. B; 2. A; 3. A; 4. A

Page 13
Day 1: 1. A; 2. B; 3. Answers will vary but
may include par, part, men, a;
Day 2: 1. A; 2. B; 3. B;
Day 3: 1. B; 2. A; 3. B;
Day 4: 1. A; 2. B; 3. A

Page 14
1. B; 2. A; 3. A; 4. Answers will vary but
may include lots of space in between
homes,
have yards

Page 15
Day 1: 1. B; 2. A; 3. A;
Day 2: 1. B; 2. B; 3. B;
Day 3: 1. B; 2. A; 3. Check students'
drawings;
Day 4: 1. B; 2. A; 3. Answers will vary.

Page 16
1. B; 2. A; 3. B; 4. Check students'
drawings.

Page 17
Day 1: 1. B; 2. A; 3. B;
Day 2: 1. A; 2. B; 3. Check students'
drawings;
Day 3: 1. B; 2. B; 3. B;
Day 4: 1. A; 2. B; 3. Cody and his dad sell
the apples.

Page 18
1. B; 2. A; 3. green; 4. Answers will vary.

Answer Key

Page 19
Day 1: 1. A; 2. A; 3. B;
Day 2: 1. A; 2. A; 3. Check students' drawings;
Day 3: 1. B; 2. C; 3. Answers will vary;
Day 4: 1. B; 2. B; 3. white, orange

Page 20
1. B; 2. A; 3. A; 4. B

Page 21
Day 1: 1. B; 2. A; 3. A;
Day 2: 1. A; 2. B; 3. B;
Day 3: 1. A; 2. B; 3. Answers will vary;
Day 4: 1. A; 2. B; 3. B

Page 22
1. B; 2. A; 3. A; 4. Check students' drawings.

Page 23
Day 1: 1. A; 2. A; 3. B;
Day 2: 1. B; 2. A; 3. B;
Day 3: 1. B; 2. A; 3. Check students' drawings;
Day 4: 1. A; 2. B; 3. A

Page 24
1. B; 2. A; 3. B; 4. Check students' drawings.

Page 25
Day 1: 1. B; 2. Check students' drawings; 3. Answers will vary;
Day 2: 1. B; 2. A; 3. B;
Day 3: 1. B; 2. A; 3. 2, 3, 1;
Day 4: 1. B; 2. A; 3. B

Page 26
1. A; 2. B; 3. A; 4. B

Page 27
Day 1: 1. B; 2. A; 3. B;
Day 2: 1. A; 2. B; 3. A;
Day 3: 1. A; 2. B; 3. Check students' drawings;
Day 4: 1. B; 2. A; 3. B

Page 28
1. B; 2. B; 3. one; 4. Check students' pictures.

Page 29
Day 1: 1. B; 2. A; 3. A;
Day 2: 1. A; 2. B; 3. A;
Day 3: 1. B; 2. A; 3. B;
Day 4: 1. A; 2. B; 3. B

Page 30
1. B; 2. A; 3. B; 4. B

CD-104595 • © Carson-Dellosa

Page 31
Day 1: 1. B; 2. B; 3. A;
Day 2: 1. A; 2. Check students' drawings; 3. B;
Day 3: 1. B; 2. B; 3. Answers will vary;
Day 4: 1. B; 2. A; 3. Answers will vary.

Page 32
1. A; 2. A; 3. B; 4. Check students' drawings

Page 33
Day 1: 1. A; 2. B; 3. B;
Day 2: 1. B; 2. A; 3. A;
Day 3: 1. B; 2. A; 3. B;
Day 4: 1. B; 2. A; 3. Check students' drawings.

Page 34
1. B; 2. B; 3. A; 4. A

Page 35
Day 1: 1. B; 2. B; 3. B;
Day 2: 1. B; 2. B; 3. A;
Day 3: 1. A; 2. A; 3. B;
Day 4: 1. A; 2. B; 3. B

Page 36
1. B; 2. B; 3. A; 4. Check students' drawings.

Page 37
Day 1: 1. A; 2. B; 3. Answers will vary;
Day 2: 1. A; 2. B; 3. B;
Day 3: 1. B; 2. A; 3. Answers will vary but may include milk and cheese;
Day 4: 1. A; 2. A; 3. Check students' drawings

Page 38
1. A; 2. B; 3. A; 4. Check students' drawings.

Page 39
Day 1: 1. B; 2. A; 3. A;
Day 2: 1. A; 2. B; 3. B;
Day 3: 1. A; 2. Check students' drawings; 3. B;
Day 4: 1. A; 2. B; 3. Check students' drawings.

Page 40
1. B; 2. A; 3. become active; 4. Check students' drawings

Page 41
Day 1: 1. B; 2. B; 3. B;
Day 2: 1. A; 2. B; 3. A;
Day 3: 1. A; 2. A; 3. B;
Day 4: 1. B; 2. B; 3. Check students' drawings.

Page 42
1. B; 2. A; 3. B; 4. Check students' drawings.

Page 43
Day 1: 1. B; 2. B; 3. B;
Day 2: 1. B; 2. A; 3. Check students' drawings;
Day 3: 1. B; 2. B; 3. A;
Day 4: 1. A; 2. B; 3. Answers will vary.

Page 44
1. B; 2. C; 3. Check students' drawings; 4. Answers will vary.

Page 45
Day 1: 1. A; 2. A; 3. C;
Day 2: 1. A; 2. A; 3. A;
Day 3: 1. A; 2. B; 3. B;
Day 4: 1. A; 2. Answers will vary but may include lay or make; 3. B

Page 46
1. A; 2. A; 3. A; 4. Answers will vary.

Page 47
Day 1: 1. B; 2. B; 3. A;
Day 2: 1. B; 2. B; 3. A;
Day 3: 1. B; 2. B; 3. Answers will vary;
Day 4: 1. B; 2. A; 3. A

Page 48
1. B; 2. B; 3. B; 4. B

Page 49
Day 1: 1. B; 2. Answers will vary; 3. Answers will vary but may include boats and ferries;
Day 2: 1. A; 2. B; 3. B;
Day 3: 1. B; 2. B; 3. Check students' drawings;
Day 4: 1. B; 2. B; 3. A

Page 50
1. A; 2. B; 3. A; 4. A

Page 51
Day 1: 1. B; 2. Check students' drawings; 3. A;
Day 2: 1. B; 2. A; 3. A;
Day 3: 1. B; 2. A; 3. A;
Day 4: 1. A; 2. A; 3. A

Page 52
1. A; 2. B; 3. A; 4. Check students' drawings.

CD-104595 • © Carson-Dellosa

Page 53

Day 1: 1. A; 2. B; 3. Check students' drawings;

Day 2: 1. A; 2. B; 3. B;

Day 3: 1. A; 2. B; 3. A;

Day 4: 1. B; 2. A; 3. Check students' drawings.

Page 54

1. B; 2. B; 3. B; 4. Answers will vary.

Page 55

Day 1: 1. B; 2. A; 3. A;

Day 2: 1. B; 2. A; 3. B;

Day 3: 1. B; 2. A; 3. A;

Day 4: 1. B; 2. A; 3. B

Page 56

1. B; 2. A; 3. B; 4. Check students' drawings.

Page 57

Day 1: 1. B; 2. B; 3. A;

Day 2: 1. B; 2. A; 3. A;

Day 3: 1. B; 2. Check students' drawings; 3. B;

Day 4: 1. B; 2. A; 3. B

Page 58

1. B; 2. A; 3. B; 4. B

Page 59

Day 1: 1. B; 2. A; 3. B;

Day 2: 1. B; 2. B; 3. Answers will vary;

Day 3: 1. B; 2. A; 3. Answers will vary;

Day 4: 1. B; 2. B; 3. B

Page 60

1. B; 2. B; 3. B; 4. Answers will vary.

Page 61

Day 1: 1. A; 2. B; 3. B;

Day 2: 1. B; 2. A; 3. A;

Day 3: 1. B; 2. B; 3. A;

Day 4: 1. B; 2. down;

3. Check students' drawings.

Page 62

1. B; 2. A; 3. B; 4. Answers will vary.

Page 63

Day 1: 1. B; 2. B; 3. B;

Day 2: 1. B; 2. B; 3. B;

Day 3: 1. A; 2. A; 3. A;

Day 4: 1. A; 2. B; 3. A

Page 64

1. B; 2. A; 3. A; 4. B

Page 65
Day 1: 1. B; 2. A; 3. Check students' drawings; **Day 2:** 1. B; 2. B; 3. Answers will vary;
Day 3: 1. A; 2. B; 3. B;
Day 4: 1. B; 2. A; 3. white

Page 66
1. B; 2. A; 3. B; 4. Answers will vary.

Page 67
Day 1: 1. B; 2. A; 3. Answers will vary;
Day 2: 1. B; 2. Answers will vary; 3. Answers will vary;
Day 3: 1. B; 2. B; 3. Answers will vary;
Day 4: 1. B; 2. A; 3. A

Page 68
1. B; 2. A; 3. B; 4. B

Page 69
Day 1: 1. B; 2. B; 3. B;
Day 2: 1. B; 2. A; 3. Answers will vary;
Day 3: 1. B; 2. A; 3. B;
Day 4: 1. B; 2. A; 3. Check students' drawings.

Page 70
1. A; 2. B; 3. B; 4. Check students' drawings.

Page 71
Day 1: 1. A; 2. B; 3. Answers will vary;
Day 2: 1. B; 2. A; 3. Check students' drawings;
Day 3: 1. B;
2. B; 3. Check students' drawings;
Day 4: 1. B;
2. A; 3. Answers will vary.

Page 72
1. B; 2. A; 3. A; 4. Check students' drawings.

Page 73
Day 1: 1. B; 2. A; 3. A;
Day 2: 1. B; 2. B; 3. Check students' drawings;
Day 3: 1. B; 2. A; 3. B;
Day 4: 1. B; 2. B; 3. A

Page 74
1. B; 2. A; 3. A; 4. Check students' drawings.

Page 75
Day 1: 1. B; 2. B; 3. Check students' drawings;
Day 2: 1. B; 2. A; 3. B;
Day 3: 1. B; 2. leaves;
3. Check students' drawings;
Day 4: 1. B; 2. A;
3. A

Page 76
1. B; 2. A; 3. B; 4. B

Page 77
Day 1: 1. B; 2. B; 3. B;
Day 2: 1. B; 2. A; 3. A;
Day 3: 1. A; 2. B; 3. Answers will vary;
Day 4: 1. B; 2. Jumpy; 3. B

Page 78
1. B; 2. A; 3. B; 4. Answers will vary.

Page 79
Day 1: 1. B; 2. A; 3. B;
Day 2: 1. B; 2. B; 3. Check students' drawings;
Day 3: 1. B; 2. B; 3. Check students' drawings;
Day 4: 1. B; 2. B; 3. A

Page 80
1. B; 2. B; 3. A; 4. cow/milk, hen/eggs

Page 81
Day 1: 1. B; 2. B; 3. B;
Day 2: 1. B; 2. A; 3. A;
Day 3: 1. A; 2. B; 3. Check students' drawings;
Day 4: 1. B; 2. A; 3. B

Page 82
1. B; 2. Check students' circling; 3. B; 4. Check students' drawings

Page 83
Day 1: 1. B; 2. B; 3. Answers will vary;
Day 2: 1. A; 2. B; 3. Check students' drawings;
Day 3: 1. B;
2. B; 3. B;
Day 4: 1. A; 2. B; 3. A

Page 84
1. B; 2. A; 3. B; 4. Check students' drawings

Page 85
Day 1: 1. B; 2. B; 3. A;
Day 2: 1. A; 2. B; 3. Answers will vary;
Day 3: 1. A; 2. B; 3. Check students'
drawings;
Day 4: 1. B; 2. B; 3. A

Page 86
1. B; 2. B; 3. A; 4. Answers will vary.

Page 87
Day 1: 1. A; 2. B; 3. Answers will vary but
may include making new friends or
sleeping in a tent;
Day 2: 1. A; 2. B; 3. Check students'
drawings;
Day 3: 1. A; 2. B; 3. A;
Day 4: 1. B; 2. B; 3. A

Page 88
1. A; 2. A; 3. B; 4. Check students'
drawings